BJ PENN

By John Hamilton

Printed in the United States of America, North Mankato, Minnesota.
052010
092010

 PRINTED ON RECYCLED PAPER

Editor: Sue Hamilton
Graphic Design: John Hamilton
Cover Photo: AP Images
Interior Photos: AP Images, p. 2, 16-17, 18-19, 19 (inset), 26-27, 28-29, 30-31; Getty Images, p. 6-7, 14-15, 24-25, 32; Ray Kasprowicz, p. 1, 3, 4-5, 8-9, 20 (inset), 20-21, 22 (inset), 22-23; Arnold Lim, p. 12-13; Dave Mandel, p. 10, 11.

Library of Congress Cataloging-in-Publication Data

Hamilton, John, 1959-
  B.J. Penn / John Hamilton.
     p. cm. -- (Xtreme UFC)
  Includes index.
  ISBN 978-1-61613-477-8
  1. Penn, B. J. 2. Martial artists--United States--Biography--Juvenile literature. I. Title.
  GV1113.P44H36 2011
  796.8092--dc22
  [B]
                          2010018545

CONTENTS

BJ

BJ Penn is a Hawaiian mixed martial artist known as "The Prodigy." His natural fighting ability has led to a long and successful career. He is a former Ultimate Fighting Championship (UFC) lightweight and welterweight champion. His speed, power, and flexibility give him excellent submission and standup skills.

PENN

At UFC 94, on January 31, 2009, Penn faced dangerous Canadian Georges St-Pierre. After four hard-fought rounds, Penn lost the match. But The Prodigy would return.

Xtreme Fight

FIGHTER

Name: BJ Penn

Nickname: The Prodigy

Born: Kailua, Hawaii, December 13, 1978

Height: 5 feet, 9 inches (1.8 m)

Weight: 155 pounds (70 kg)

Nationality: American

Division: Lightweight—146 to 155 pounds (66 to 70 kg)

Reach: 70 inches (178 cm)

Fighting Style: Brazilian jiu-jitsu, boxing

Fighting Out Of: Hilo, Hawaii

Martial Arts Rank: Black belt in Brazilian jiu-jitsu

Mixed Martial Arts Record (as of April 2010)

  Total Fights: 22

  Wins: 15 (6 by knockout, 6 by submission, 3 by decision)

  Losses: 6

  Draws: 1

STATS

RECORD

BJ Penn's UFC Fight Record (including The Ultimate Fighter 5)

Event	Date	Result	Opponent	Method
UFC 112	4/10/2010	Loss	Frankie Edgar	Unanimous Decision
UFC 107	12/12/2009	Win	Diego Sanchez	Technical Knockout
UFC 101	8/8/2009	Win	Kenny Florian	Submission
UFC 94	1/31/2009	Loss	Georges St-Pierre	Technical Knockout
UFC 84	5/24/2008	Win	Sean Sherk	Technical Knockout
UFC 80	1/19/2008	Win	Joe Stevenson	Submission
TUF 5	6/23/2007	Win	Jens Pulver	Submission
UFC 63	9/23/2006	Loss	Matt Hughes	Technical Knockout
UFC 58	3/4/2006	Loss	Georges St-Pierre	Split Decision
UFC 46	1/31/2004	Win	Matt Hughes	Submission
UFC 41	2/28/2003	Draw	Caol Uno	Draw
UFC 39	9/27/2002	Win	Matt Serra	Unanimous Decision
UFC 37	5/10/2002	Win	Paul Creighton	Technical Knockout
UFC 35	1/11/2002	Loss	Jens Pulver	Majority Decision
UFC 34	11/2/2001	Win	Caol Uno	Knock Out
UFC 32	6/29/2001	Win	Din Thomas	Technical Knockout
UFC 31	5/4/2001	Win	Joey Gilbert	Technical Knockout

UFC = Ultimate Fighting Championship
TUF = *The Ultimate Fighter*

FIGHT

TRAINING

Xtreme Fact

BJ Penn trains with a strength and conditioning coach in his hometown of Hilo, Hawaii. He brings in top fighters from around the country to help him train and spar.

BJ Penn was introduced to Brazilian jiu-jitsu when he was 17 by a neighbor in his hometown of Hilo, Hawaii. By 2000, he earned his black belt. That year, he won the World Jiu-Jitsu Championship in Rio de Janeiro, Brazil. He was the first non-Brazilian to win the black belt division.

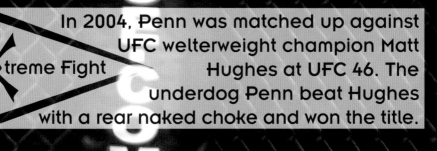

In 2004, Penn was matched up against UFC welterweight champion Matt Hughes at UFC 46. The underdog Penn beat Hughes with a rear naked choke and won the title.

UFC 63
Vs. Matt
Hughes

At UFC 63 on September 23, 2006, Penn fought a rematch against Matt Hughes. Penn controlled the fight for the first two rounds. But after suffering a rib injury, Penn slowed down. During the third round, Hughes won by TKO and took back the welterweight title.

UFC 80 Vs. Joe Stevenson

After coaching *The Ultimate Fighter 5* on Spike TV, Penn moved down to the lightweight division. On January 19, 2008, he defeated Joe Stevenson to win the UFC Lightweight Championship. It's very rare for fighters to win championships in two weight classes, but Penn had the talent to do it.

Vs. Sean Sherk

Penn defended his lightweight title against former champion Sean Sherk at UFC 84 on May 24, 2008. It was a stand-up battle, with Penn throwing a flurry of jabs, uppercuts, and hooks. After three rounds, Penn won the fight by technical knockout.

UFC 94 Vs. Georges St-Pierre

On January 31, 2009, Penn moved up a weight class to welterweight. He wanted to avenge his earlier loss to champion Georges St-Pierre. During the first two rounds, Penn used counterstrikes and excellent takedown defense against St-Pierre.

Bitter Defeat

In the final two rounds of UFC 94, Penn's energy faded. St-Pierre punished the challenger with punches and a devastating ground-and-pound attack. Penn lost by technical knockout after four rounds. The loss made Penn more determined than ever to train harder and defend his lightweight title.

UFC 101 Vs. Kenny Florian

On August 8, 2009, Penn defended his lightweight title against Kenny Florian. This time, Penn paced himself. He punished the challenger with bursts of striking and powerful takedowns. Penn won by submission with a rear naked choke in the fourth round.

UFC 107 Vs. Diego Sanchez

Defending his lightweight title for the third time, Penn faced Diego Sanchez on December 12, 2009. Sanchez was a scrappy challenger, but he was no match for Penn's lightning-fast punches and high kicks. Penn won in round five with a technical knockout.

UFC 112 Vs. Frankie Edgar

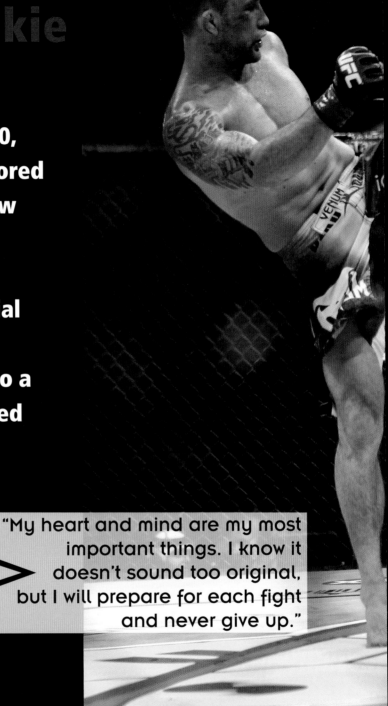

On April 10, 2010, the heavily favored Penn lost to New Jersey native Frankie Edgar. The controversial decision may someday lead to a much-anticipated rematch.

Xtreme Quote

"My heart and mind are my most important things. I know it doesn't sound too original, but I will prepare for each fight and never give up."

Brazilian Jiu-Jitsu
A fighting style made popular by fighters from Brazil that specializes in grappling and ground fighting, including chokes and joint locks.

Decision
If a match finishes without a clear victor, either by knockout or submission, a panel of three judges decides the winner. If only two judges agree on the winner, it is called a split decision.

Ground and Pound
A style of fighting where an opponent is taken down and then punched or submitted.

Jab
A strike used in boxing and karate. When in a fighting stance, the lead fist is thrown straight out. Jabs are not as powerful as regular punches, but they are very quick and effective.

GLOSSARY

Kickboxing
A style of fighting that relies mainly on a mix of kicking and punching. Muay Thai is a type of kickboxing that is the national sport of Thailand.

Mixed Martial Arts
A full-contact sport that allows a mix of different martial arts, such as boxing, karate, and wrestling. The most popular mixed martial arts (MMA) organization is the Ultimate Fighting Championship (UFC).

Octagon
The eight-sided ring in which Ultimate Fighting Championship fighters compete.

Uppercut
A strike used in boxing and karate that starts low and sweeps upward, often connecting with an opponent's chin. It is often a match-ending strike.

INDEX